BITS & PIECES

One of the delights of using fabrics and threads is the shopping. We may not need much excuse for browsing, though a full purse or a plastic card is a temptation to spend.

Having seen the price I would have to pay in a craft shop for a packet of about 10 silver washers, I wondered how this would compare to what I could buy them for in a DIY shop.

The small town hardware shop is a delightful place to browse, but often enough helpful assistants will seek to give advice or find things for us. The most awkward question is then "What do you want it for?" Unless you have a clear idea, it is often best to start looking in one of the DIY chains. Here you can pick up the packs of washers (in various sizes) which you came in for, as well as study the shelves for other things which may inspire you. You don't have to know what things are used for. Tile spacers may be obvious, but little clips and ties perhaps less so.

The following pages show patterns which can be created just by applying these DIY bits. As soon as you start to add other stitches or areas of paint, their origin becomes less obvious and they start to take on a life of their own.

To Denise
Enjoy Doing It
Yourself
Best wishes Victoria MacLeod

Washers, nuts, tile spacers, wire staples and cotton washing line – with the addition of Fly Stitch, Chain Stitch and Cross Stitch.

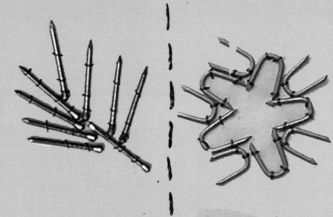

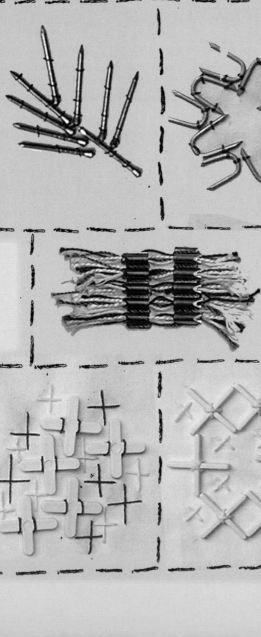

WASHERS

Washers come in various sizes and are measured in millimetres across. You can get them in silver or brass. Try various ways of stitching them down: fly stitch, chain stitch, cross stitch or just plain straight stitch – Try varying the number of stitches or the length of stitches.

NUTS

Nuts can be quite heavy if you apply too many but they do fit together nicely because they're hexagonal.

NAILS

Nails can be arranged in a variety of ways. They have to be stitched down quite tightly, otherwise they may fall out! Copper nails are particularly attractive.

WIRE STAPLES

These metal pieces hold cables in place but can be arranged in circles so that they radiate and create a feeling of movement and expansion. When put in lines they form a loopy effect and this can be enhanced with loopy stitches.

TILE SPACERS

These are little plastic crosses and come in packs of a hundred or so. They can be painted before being applied in various ways to background fabric .
(see greetings cards on page19)

BUY AND TRY

Just buy packets of things to experiment with. At first I thought these Corr Nails were clips for wires, but I think that they are really for hammering into joined wooden corners to strengthen them. Any way, after you've stitched them down you can run threads through them.

Opposite: Sampler – from top to bottom
Nuts and herringbone stitch
String couched with cross stitch
Alternating wire staples couched with straight sts
Silver washers with shared stitches
Couched hemp
Thin tile spacers
Larger washers
Shisha glass and nails
Thick tile spacers

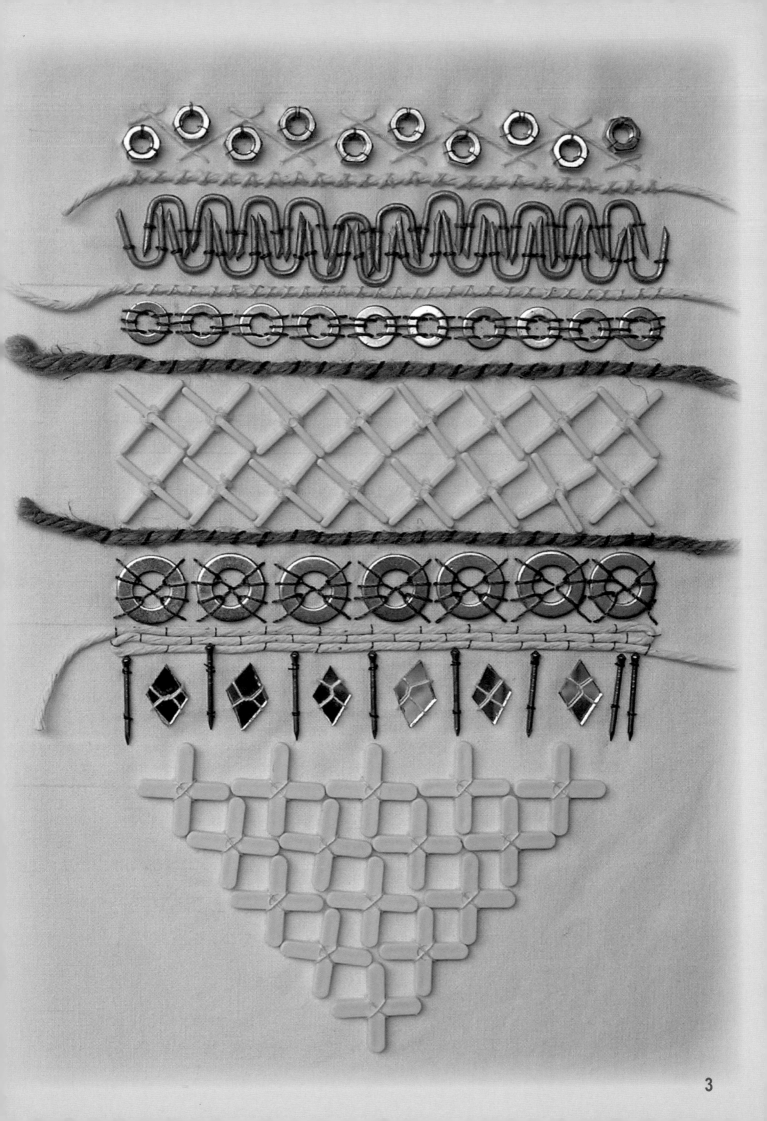

THICK THREADS

The DIY shop is also a good source of cords, cables and tubing. They are not elegant and certainly not designed for going through fabric, but they can be couched down as they are, covered with fabric, or wrapped round with thread, laid between two pieces of fabric (like quilting), chopped into bits or segments, distorted or frayed – and of course PAINTED.

STRING

Jute, hemp, synthetic twine, rope. Couch it down, do fancy stitches over it, cover it with crusty beads, put knots in it.

CORDS

Look in the curtaining section for interesting twisted effects and unusual colours.

CABLES

Electrical cables have wires inside and this means that you can twist them into interesting shapes. Alternatively you can split them and take out individual wires – bend and apply, stitch with, knit with.
(see fireworks card on page 19)

PIPES AND TUBES

These may be either rigid or flexible depending upon their use. Plumbers' piping is usually rigid and not always made of copper. Some of the plastic stuff can be used to support fabric or hangings vertically or horizontally by pushing it through a hem.

HOSE PIPE

This is much more flexible and can be wrapped with thread, wool or string, ribbon or fabric.

Top of Page
Couched cotton-covered cord
Above
Knitted Hemp

Below
Three covered hose pipes, intertwined with washing line, washing line wrapped with raggy yarn, crocheted knitting ribbon, machine made cords, and chenille yarn.

Inset Picture
Two sizes of plastic tubing wrapped with threads dyed by Oliver Twists. Slices of tubing cut and painted to harmonise, with washers and serrated washers, couched ball chain and straight chain

Background
Split washers and jute on hessian painted with emulsion

PAINT

If you have already done quite a bit of stitching you may well have used silk paints and fabric dyes. These are essential if you are colouring a fabric which needs to retain its softness and is washable.

However, if you are decorating something which will not be worn then there are many alternatives:

Acrylic paints can be used to paint onto fabric as a background, or even paint over areas which have already been stitched. While they can be thinned with water or acrylic medium the plastic element seeps into the fibres and, once dried, will not wash out.

Emulsion paint is cheaper than acrylic, comes in a range of matt colours, is compatible with acrylic (so you can change the tone subtly yourself with the addition of acrylic paint). This too can be diluted with water (which is also used for washing out brushes).

If you have a huge area of fabric or canvas to cover you may wish to buy a normal tin, but for most purposes a range of colours is available in a trial size tin or tube and these are excellent for altering both colour and texture on fabric.

Below
Three basic samples of furnishing fabric with stitch and emulsion paint

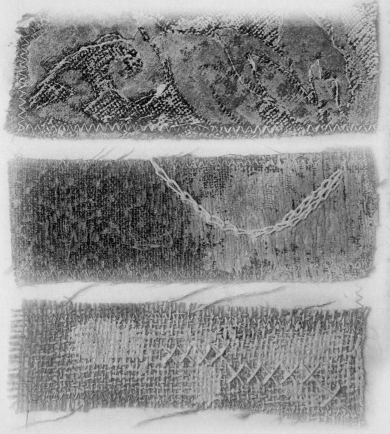

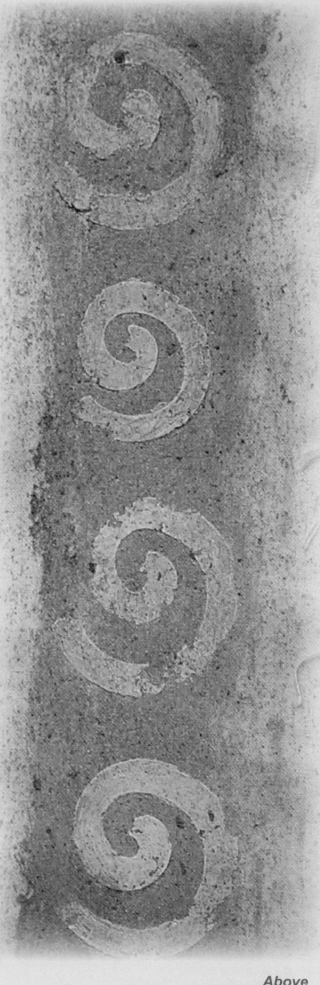

Above
Stencilled spirals of plaster and emulsion with stone effect spray paint

SPECIALIST PAINTS

The DIY shop also stocks a range of paints used to achieve special effects. In and among the emulsions for walls you will find **metallic effect**, **suede effect** and **pearl effect** paint. When applied to woven matt fabric rather than a hard non-porous surface like a wall, they will not be quite as shiny, but some of the shearer fabrics which are not quite so absorbent will give a more luminous effect.

In another section you will find cans of **spray paint.** These are very easy to apply to fabrics, though inevitably make them stiffer in texture.

Be careful with those which are 'enamel' or designed for use on cars as they are designed to have a particularly hard surface and will alter the quality of your fabric significantly (which you may want!)

Be cautious when using spray paint because of chemical fumes. Spray in a well-ventilated area and try to wear a protective mask.

An interesting spray paint to use is a **stone effect** or speckled one. This adds more than one colour and texture at the same time and is excellent for stitching between the speckles with French knots or little beads when dry.

Webbing spray can add a distressed worn look and the black, gold and silver can be used to good effect. It may not adhere well to fabric before it has been painted. For best results, hold the can well back from the surface (30-40 cm away).

Crackle glazes are interesting to use but need to be applied to non-porous surfaces such as wood, metal, plastic or card. These can then be applied to fabric. You may also consider this effect as a frame or border around your stitching.

Remember that you do not have to apply paint in one coat. Some of the best effects are obtained by applying minimal paint with a dryish brush or sponge, allowing it to dry, and stitching into it.

Even that may not be the end effect, as stitches which have been painted show a different quality which highlights the texture. Stitching on top of them will bring back more colour.

You do need some patience though – to wait for the paint to dry before stitching again!

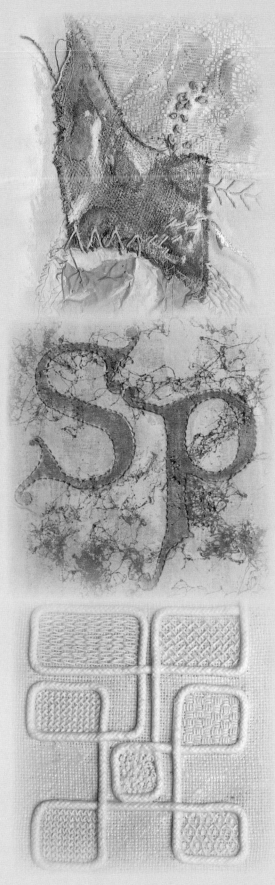

Top
Lace, furnishing fabric and curtain lining, painted with cream emulsion and blue acrylic

Middle
Shapes cut out of stiff interfacing between 2 layers of cotton, painted with light emulsion and gold pva, with gold webbing spray

Bottom
Cotton-covered cord with neutral cotton stitches, painted with pearlised household paint

Stitch

and paint

and stitch

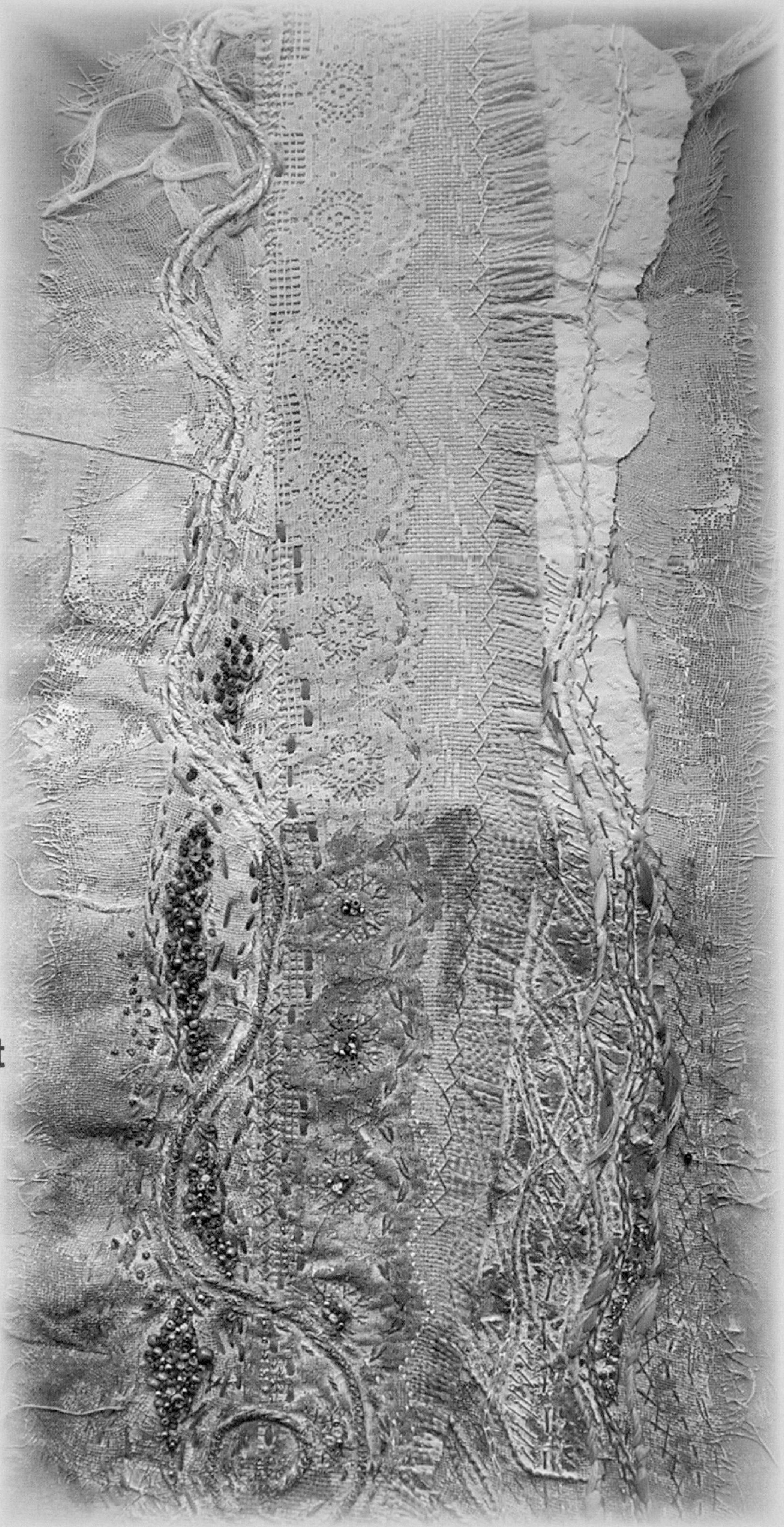

and paint

and stitch

8

INCORPORATING PAPER AND CARD

If your embroidery is purely for decorative purposes and not to be worn or washed or needing to be soft and flexible, you can add texture with paper and card. You will find that they take the paint more easily than fabric, though you have to be careful with the stitching as any mistakes show as holes.

Hand made paper adds wonderful texture, but can be a little fragile when stitched into.

Brown envelope paper can be scrunched up and painted with acrylic paint. Try wetting the paper first. The addition of a polish or varnish over the top will give a mock leather effect.

(Blue sample on right)

Tissue paper can be used to good effect, pasted on paper or fabric. As with any scrunched paper the paint is taken up unevenly and gives a lovely veined texture. It is so soft that it can be moulded around padding or card shapes.

(Sample on right is green tissue paper over craft interfacing shapes with a black acrylic wash and gold rub-on applied when dry)

Corrugated card gives the effect of tucks and ripples.

(Sample below has been painted with green and copper acrylic paint, stitched with string, tissue on card medallions added, painted wallpaper added and given a final irregular coating of bronze paint)

GALLERY

Rug canvas stitched onto calico and then brushed with metallic paints. Washers, wire, curtain hooks and eyes attached on top

Kathleen Thompson

Spray dyed fabric and lace dyed silver. Nuts, washers, wire staples, cable clips and cotton cord added.

Victoria MacLeod

Black plastic refuse sack bonded onto calico and used as a background. Black cable ties wrapped with wire couched onto the surface and washers, chains and metallic painted plastic tubing added on top.

Kathleen Thompson

Wallpaper, emulsion, print and stitch blended.

Maggie Smith

Calico painted with metallic paint, layers of painted wallpaper bonded onto the surface. Washers and links added onto surface.

Kathleen Thompson

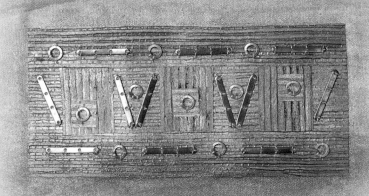

Plastic garden mesh, painted with brown and copper acrylic paint. Metal washers suspended in the spaces by wrapping and looping knitting ribbon

Victoria MacLeod

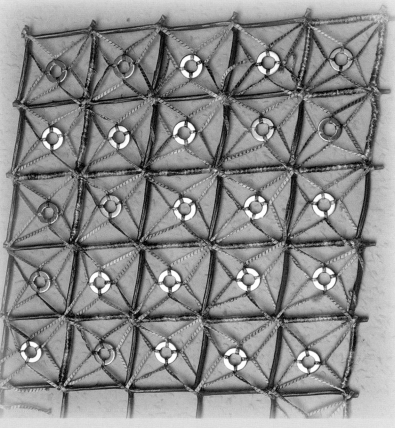

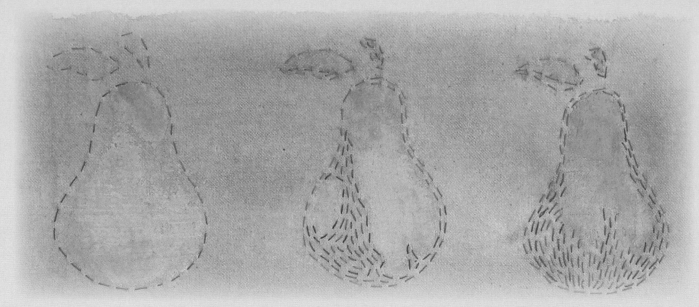

SHAPE SHIFTING

There are so many things around at the moment which can help you apply or repeat a shape accurately.

STENCILS

In the DIY shops there are **stencils** to buy which may be used for applying paint to borders around rooms or items of painted furniture. They are usually made of plastic and can be used many times.

You can use them to stencil onto fabric or paper using fabric dye, acrylic paint, emulsion paint or some kind of resist such as wax, flour paste or plaster/filler.

Do be careful that you do not apply a very fluid paint or dye through a stencil onto untreated fabric. The colour will simply bleed into the fibres and leave you with a smudge. If applying directly onto fabric then treat it first, either with a spray stiffener, or with a neutral emulsion or gesso.

You can use ordinary masking tape to mask off areas of your design where you don't want paint or dye to go. This is really limited to straight-line designs. When using liquid paints and curvy designs, then applying gutta to the outline will confine the colour to where you want it.

Top of page
Stencilled plaster shapes sponge-painted and then surface stitched.

Above right
Emulsion paint and acrylic applied through zig zag stencil with herringbone stitch and straight stitches added.

Right
Filler stencilled onto coarse weave fabric, washed with purple dye and embroidered with couched knitting threads.

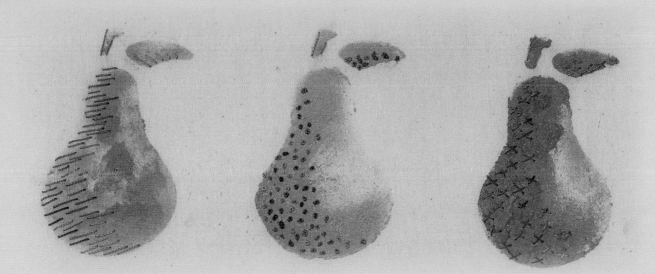

STAMPING

There are so many stamps around at the moment, many of which are suitable only for use on paper. The bolder patterned ones which are made of foam on a foam or rubber block are the most suitable for applying directly to fabric. Again, fluid, runny paints will bleed into the fibres but paint with more body, such as emulsion or acrylic will stay on the surface.

You can make your own stamps to do original printing by using craft foam, polystyrene or even card, cut to shape and stuck to a backing of card or wood.

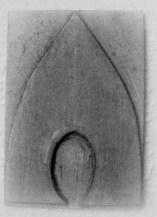

Top of page
Grey acrylic paint with straight stitches, acrylic paint with added sand and French knots, and acrylic paint with added snipped fibres and cross stitches.

Above right
Two stamps created by Maggie Smith from card and string, inspired by line drawings of Egyptian friezes.

Above left
Maggie's experiment with the stamps on paper.

Right
Maggie's experiment with the stamps on fabric

WALLPAPER

Wallpaper may be seen as an unlikely material to use in embroidery, but it can be a quick and easy way of adding texture or pattern to a large or small area within the stitching.

It is not advisable to use too great an area for a background which may require a lot of stitching into. It is harder to push a needle through than plain fabric, especially if it is also painted. If the needle is pushed through in the wrong place accidentally then a permanent hole is made (which can usually be pushed back a little).

Machine stitching is easier but you will need to clean inside your machine frequently as a lot of paper dust is generated.

For your personal use you can sometimes utilise paper which has quite a distinctive pattern – especially if it is something to be hung in a room to complement the décor. Be careful if doing something like this commercially as you may fall foul of copyright issues.

Ordinary textured white or cream wallpaper forms an excellent base for playing around with. Be aware that some of the texturing is achieved with a layer of polystyrene or other meltable plastic – so you need to exercise caution if you have to iron it or heat it up at all.

SAMPLES
This Page - Cylindrical vessels by Ros Murphy
1 – Yarns and ribbons stitched to the surface of unpainted wallpaper. Small washers inserted into the ribbon before stitching. Circles punched from the wallpaper stitched in place to complement the washers. Plasticised metallic fabric glued to reverse before making a cylinder
2 – Red, yellow and orange dyes applied to the surface with second layer in green and turquoise, then gold poster paint added on top. The raised surface does not take the dyes as well as the background paper. Cylinder was attached using electrical components through regularly punched holes.
3 – Blue dye onto surface with beads made of rolled wallpaper added for decoration.
4 – Metallic paint with brads of similar colour to secure the cylinder.
Opposite page by Ros Murphy and Kathleen Thompson

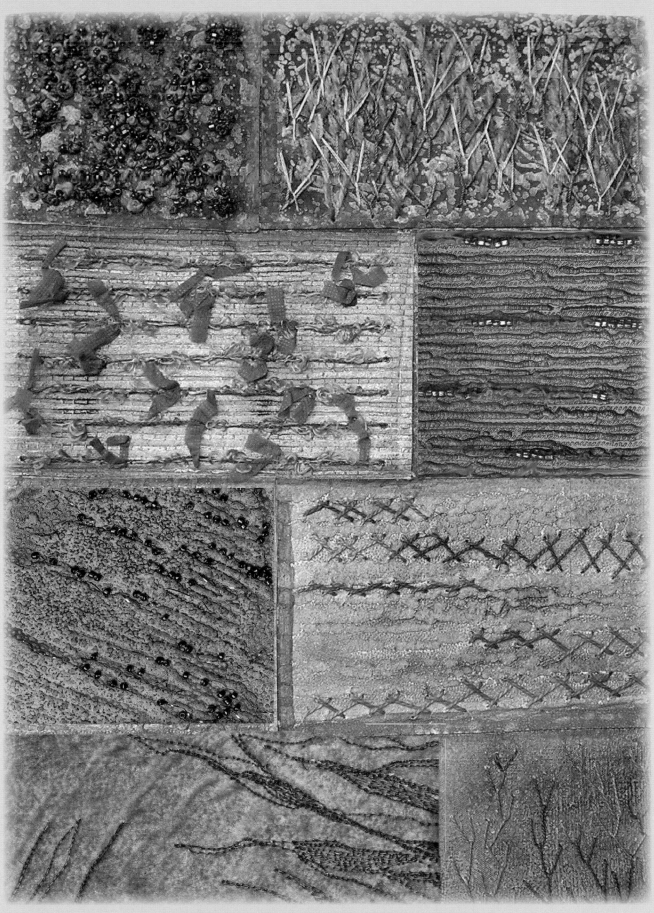

Painted wallpapers bonded onto calico:

1. With French knots and beads (KT)
2. Fly Stitch (KT)
3. Metallic rub-ons with couched threads (KT)
4. Wrapped with space-dyed yarn + beads (RM)
5. Beads applied to accentuate ridges (RM)
6. Herringbone Stitch (KT)
7. Dyed abaca paper applied to textured paper, dilute pva glue used to press into contours, rub on metallics (RM)
8. Feather Stitch (KT)

Lining paper can be a good alternative to a sketchbook if you have to map out a particularly large design.

Polystyrene lining paper can be drawn on with a free-running ball point pen and then etched into with a stencil/heat tool. It can then be either painted or overlaid with fabric.

Right
Polystyrene, sprayed with speckled copper paint, stitched to a contrasting fabric with brass washers and counter sinks added

Above

Glue gun applied to celtic pattern stitched on corrugated card, then painted with emulsion

Right
Background of metallic painted wallpaper, bonded onto calico. Additional shapes cut from wallpaper, painted with wood varnish, bonded onto background and couched with jack chains and curb chains.
Kathleen Thompson

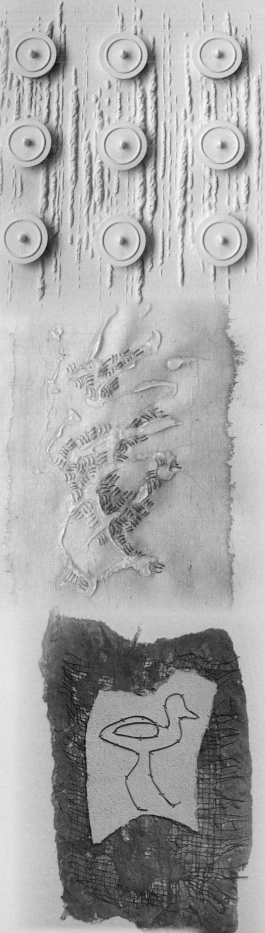

Simple wire shape attached to the top of painted fabric stiffener, with builders' scrim in the background

OFF THE SHELF

PLASTER AND FILLER

Use for adding texture to the surface of fabric, either before or after stitching, or for coating mistakes (plastering over the cracks!). Make up the filler with water and then add PVA glue and emulsion paint. For a whole host of ideas, look at the companion book to this ('Get Plastered' by Maggie Smith) *Stitched and couched threads coated with plaster. Bath plugs added. Maggie Smith*

PVA

PVA is sold in DIY shops in larger containers than those found in Art and Craft shops. It is also stronger in concentration than craft glue (especially the stuff made for use by children) and so sticks more efficiently. You will need to look in craft shops for pva mediums which add texture. Or you can add your own snippets of fabric or clean fine sand. *(See pears on page 13)*

GLUE GUN

Use a glue gun for 'piping' upraised lines (like icing a cake). You can sprinkle tiny accent beads on top or stitch either side to accentuate the effect. *Glue piped on to calico, fabric dye flooded in, in different intensities with stitching added afterwards.*

CHAINS

If you have noticed chains in a DIY store you have probably disregarded them – especially those 'zinc plated steel welded' chains which weigh in heavily at over £12 per metre! However there are other more delicate chains which could be used to add interest to textile work. Figaro chain is made of fine copper wire and costs less than £1 per metre. Look also for Ball chain, Curb chain, Belcher chain, Jack chain (single and double), Safety chain, Oval chain, Straight chain, Marquis chain, Knotted chain and Gothic chain. You might feel that they are just not appropriate for use in your work – but think about using them as a feature to hang work up *(see Kathleen Thompson's Wallpaper and Chain sample opposite).*

WIRE

Wire can be used to add structure and support to three dimensional pieces. Or it can be manipulated with pliers and attached to provide surface decoration. Electrical cable may contain several wires within an outer plastic sheath. Be careful with those wires which do not have any surface treatment as they may corrode and stain any fabrics with which they are in contact for any length of time.

BUILDERS' SCRIM AND MUSLIN

Builders' scrim is used for giving a rough surface which will take and hold plaster well. It's sold on a roll about 3 inches wide, is quite stiff and very good for adding interest to backgrounds, providing texture for paint, plaster or stitch.

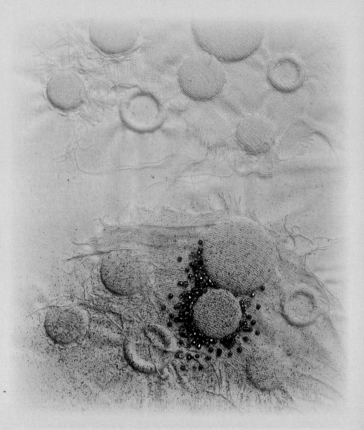

FURNITURE PROTECTORS

These come in packs of varying shapes and sizes. They can be stuck onto background fabric, covered over and stitched around to add raised texture similar to quilting.

(Sample on right shows furniture protectors and curtain rings underneath muslin. The bottom sample is sprayed with stone effect paint and has beads added.)

CURTAIN RINGS AND LOOPS

These come in various sizes and thickness. You can cover with a layer of fabric as described above, or wrap them round with strips of fabric or threads before applying them to a background fabric. Secure them in position by stitching over, then wrap around the ring only a few times before doing another securing stitch. For a really secure attachment, do a buttonhole stitch all the way around the ring, turn the knots of the stitches to the outside (as for Dorset buttons) and then stitch around and through the knots.

(Sample on right shows wrapped curtain rings and counter sinks with needle-weaving and beads.)

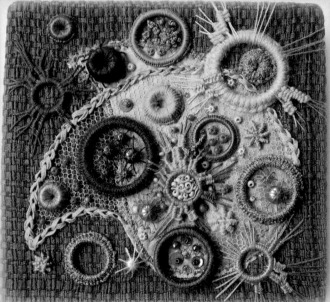

CURTAIN POLES

If you have stitched a large hanging or textile then making a loop at the top to accommodate a curtain pole may be a bold and effective way to display it. Pole ends or finials have become really ornamental and may considerably enhance your piece.

BAMBOO LENGTHS

Don't forget the Garden Centre section of your DIY shop. Bamboo canes are sold straight or curved and offer possibilities for hanging textiles on or lacing fabric round. They can be sanded, primed and painted any colour you wish.

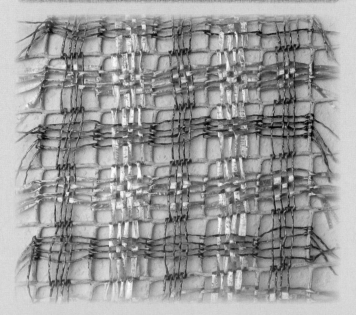

GARDEN MESHES

These can be can be woven or stitched into or used to add structure to 3-dimensional items. Try painting them first (or after!). Try weaving with strips of plastic bags or plastic tags.

(Sample on right shows mesh painted with light blue emulsion and woven with twine and raffia.)

IDEAS for GREETINGS CARDS

Some of the ideas in this book you may be able to use in your usual embroideries or textile art, but some you may just wish to try on a small scale.

Greetings cards are a fun way to justify your experiments and a few ideas are pictured on this page. Whatever you do – have some fun!!

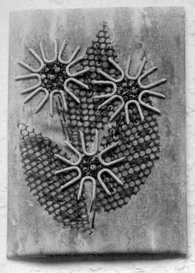

CABLE CLIPPED SUNFLOWER
Clips painted with yellow acrylic paint, applied over shapes of fine garden mesh, centres filled with wooden beads and French Knots

FIREWORK CELEBRATIONS
Electric Cable stripped and curved with the addition of sequins

ELECTRIC KISSES
Tile spacers and cross stitches with a border of electric cable

HAPPY BIRTHDAY
Balloons created by wrapping curtain rings and plumber's O rings

NUTS ABOUT YOU
Traditional Hardanger embroidery with nuts applied in the spaces

HOOKED ON YOU
Card for your Valentine using cup hooks and paper cut out hearts

YOUR TOOLBOX

HAND DRILL

Replace the bit with a cup hook. Tie your yarns around this at one end and loop round a door handle at the other. Twist the handle and make your own cords without anyone else's assistance. Don't make them too long, otherwise you'll have some difficulty getting to the middle to twist them!

ELECTRIC DRILL

Use a small, light-weight drill for making holes in found objects such as shells, small pieces of metal and plastic. You can then get a needle through to stitch them down securely.

PLIERS

Use for shaping/bending wire, making loops and spirals. Also handy when you've got a needle stuck part way through a particularly tough or thick piece of fabric. Tugging with the pliers pulls them through much more easily.

WIRE CUTTERS

Makes cutting wire easy – and saves you from blunting your scissors!

METAL RULERS

Use these whenever you need to cut anything with a sharp craft knife. Lean your stencil burning tool against them when you have to burn or incise a straight edge.

SET SQUARES

Can be metal or plastic but are indispensable when needing to get a good right angle on fabric, card or paper.

HAMMER

A hammer can be used for beating metal foil into shape, setting an eyelet into fabric, or hammering a hook into the wall in order to show your finished piece to advantage.

SCREW DRIVER/SPANNERS

Not used very often but you need to have access to if you regularly work on an embroidery frame. You can get things so much tighter by using the right tools.

SANDPAPER

A good item to have in the tool kit. Comes in various grades of coarseness. Use it for preparing surfaces for painting, adding texture to painted surfaces or for sanding off emulsion.

BRUSHES

Brushes can be very cheap in DIY shops – you can get several in a pack for a few pounds. These are ideal for using once or twice and then discarding. Be careful that they don't shed their bristles where you don't want them. Some brushes are made of polypropylene and don't 'hold' the paint as well as others, or have bristles so hard that they leave marks in the surface.